RETURN FROM EXTINCTION

THE GREEN SEA TURTLE

LEONARD CLASKY

Gareth Stevens PUBLISHING

Please visit our website, www.garethstevens.com. For a free color catalog of all our high-quality books, call toll free 1-800-542-2595 or fax 1-877-542-2596.

Portions of this work were originally authored by Melissa Raé Shofner and published as *The Return of the Green Sea Turtle.* All new material this edition authored by Leonard Clasky.

Library of Congress Cataloging-in-Publication Data

Names: Clasky, Leonard, author.
Title: The green sea turtle / Leonard Clasky.
Description: New York : Gareth Stevens Publishing, [2023] | Series: Return from extinction | Includes index.
Identifiers: LCCN 2022000799 (print) | LCCN 2022000800 (ebook) | ISBN 9781538280331 (library binding) | ISBN 9781538280317 (paperback) | ISBN 9781538280324 (set) | ISBN 9781538280348 (ebook)
Subjects: LCSH: Green turtle–Conservation–Juvenile literature. | Rare reptiles–Conservation–Juvenile literature.
Classification: LCC QL666.C536 C55 2023 (print) | LCC QL666.C536 (ebook) | DDC 597.92/8–dc23/eng/20220113
LC record available at https://lccn.loc.gov/2022000799
LC ebook record available at https://lccn.loc.gov/2022000800

Published in 2023 by
Gareth Stevens Publishing
29 E. 21st Street
New York, NY 10010

Designer: Olivia Lo Sardo
Editor: Caitie McAneney

Photo credits: Cover LaverneNash/Shutterstock; p5. EvanAusten/Shutterstock; p7. blue-sea.cz/Shutterstock; p9. WorldsWildLifeWonders/Shutterstock; p10-11 Neophutket/Shutterstock; p12. CitrusDeliciosa/Shutterstock; p13. LauraDts/Shutterstock; p15. MattJeppson/Shutterstock; p17, p12. RichCarey/Shutterstock; p18. ShaneMyers/Shutterstock; p19. RMNunes/Shutterstock; p21 EmirHankaramuk/Shutterstock; p23. https://commons.wikimedia.org/wiki/File:Turtlewithfptumors0149026.jpg; p25 JaromirChalabala/Shutterstock; p26-27 ToryKallman/Shutterstock; p29. SeaSandSun/Shutterstock

Printed in the United States of America

Some of the images in this book illustrate individuals who are models. The depictions do not imply actual situations or events.

CPSIA compliance information: Batch #CSGS23: For further information contact Gareth Stevens, New York, New York at 1-800-542-2595.

CONTENTS

Words in the glossary appear in **bold** type the first time they are used in the text.

TURTLES IN TROUBLE

Green sea turtles are one of the largest hard-shelled sea turtles on Earth. These turtles can grow to 3 to 5 feet (0.9 m to 1.5 m) long. They can also weigh 700 pounds (317.5 kg)! They swim long distances back and forth between their feeding and nesting areas. Green sea turtles play an important part in the ocean ecosystem, or community of living and nonliving things.

Green sea turtles have a **tragic** history, however. Over the past several centuries, human actions have caused green sea turtle populations to drop sharply. **Conservation** efforts have brought green sea turtle populations up—but these gentle giants are still endangered in many places.

ENDANGERED SPECIES

ENDANGERED MEANS THAT A LIVING THING IS IN DANGER OF GOING EXTINCT, OR DYING OUT. TODAY, GREEN SEA TURTLES ARE CONSIDERED ENDANGERED IN MANY PLACES. SCIENTISTS DON'T KNOW HOW MANY GREEN SEA TURTLES WERE ON EARTH WHEN THEIR POPULATIONS FIRST BEGAN TO **DECLINE**. HOWEVER, IT'S CLEAR THERE ARE FEWER ALIVE NOW THAN THERE WERE IN THE PAST.

Looking at the ways that humans have harmed green sea turtles can help people protect them.

MEET THE GREEN SEA TURTLE

Green sea turtles are also called green turtles, or simply greens. However, green sea turtles aren't usually green at first glance. Their shell may be brown, yellow, gray, or even black. Their name actually comes from a layer of green fat beneath their shell. This green coloring is thought to come from the seagrass and **algae** they eat.

Green sea turtles are found around the world in **subtropical** coastal waters. The two main types of green sea turtle are the Atlantic green turtle and the Eastern Pacific green turtle. The largest populations are found in Australia and Costa Rica.

MAKING A MOVE

GREEN SEA TURTLES MIGRATE, OR MOVE FROM PLACE TO PLACE. THESE REPTILES SPEND MUCH OF THEIR TIME IN WARM, SHALLOW COASTAL WATERS. DURING **BREEDING** SEASON, THEY'LL OFTEN SWIM LONG DISTANCES ACROSS THE OPEN OCEAN TO NESTING SITES ON LAND. THEY HAVE BEEN RECORDED TO MIGRATE MORE THAN 1,615.6 MILES (2,600 KM)!

GREEN SEA TURTLE RANGE

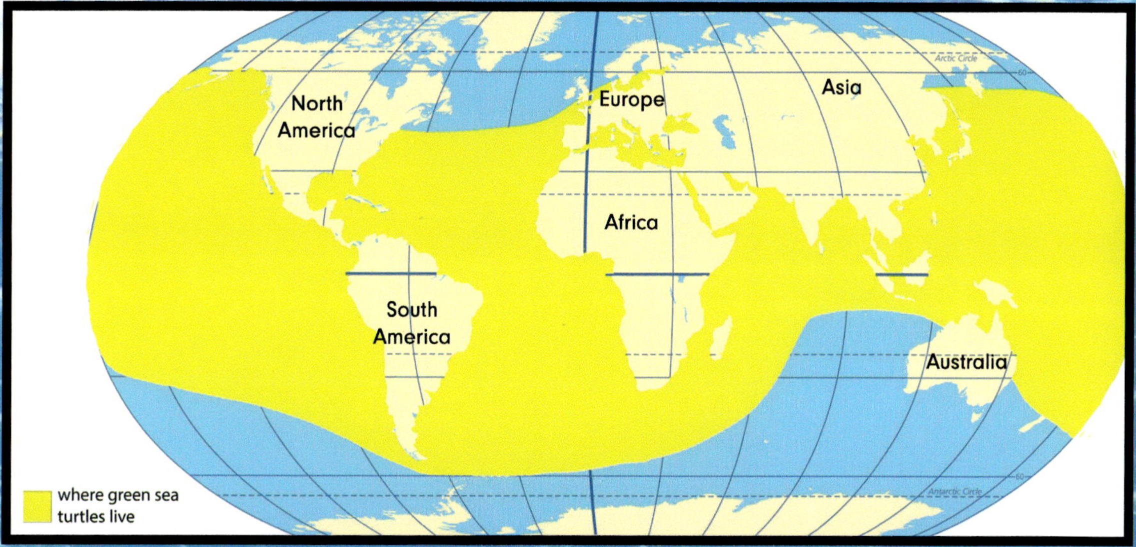

Green sea turtles have wide, smooth shells. Though large, they swim gracefully in the water.

A LOOK AT HISTORY

Native Peoples in the Pacific Islands honored the green sea turtle. In Hawaii, a chief controlled the use of turtles. Green turtles provided meat and eggs to eat, and their bones and shells were made into tools, fishhooks, and containers.

In the 1500s, European explorers in Central America saw green sea turtles for the first time. Many populations were hunted to near extinction as explorers began killing the turtles for their meat, shells, skin, and eggs. These goods were sometimes sent back to Europe. This was just the beginning of the centuries-long international turtle trade.

THE TERRIBLE TURTLE TRADE

THE SEA TURTLE CONSERVATION STRATEGY, OR PLAN, OF 1979 NOTED THAT SEA TURTLES "HAVE BEEN **OVEREXPLOITED** MOST FREQUENTLY TO FEED, CLOTHE, AND ADORN [DECORATE] THE WEALTHY IN EUROPE, NORTH AMERICA, AND EASTERN ASIA." DESPITE LAWS PLACED ON THE INTERNATIONAL TURTLE TRADE IN THE 1970S AND 1980S, MANY HARMFUL PRACTICES CONTINUED. HUNTING OF GREEN TURTLES, BOTH LEGALLY AND ILLEGALLY, IS STILL A BIG PROBLEM.

Sea turtles have lived on Earth for more than 110 million years.

ESSENTIAL TO THE ECOSYSTEM

Ecosystems are communities of creatures, plants, and nonliving things in a certain area. Each living thing depends on the others to stay balanced. If one creature suffers, other creatures suffer as well. Looking at how green sea turtles affect their ecosystem can tell scientists how their population decline might hurt the creatures around them.

Green sea turtles play an important part in their ecosystem. That's because they eat a lot of seagrass! In fact, they spend most of their time **grazing** along seagrass meadows. Like gardeners of the sea, green sea turtles keep seagrass trimmed. This keeps it healthy and growing.

SEAGRASS'S STABILIZING POWER

HEALTHY SEAGRASS CAN PREVENT SANDY OCEAN BOTTOMS FROM WASHING AWAY DURING STRONG STORMS. THIS IS BECAUSE IT HAS A LONG AND WIDE ROOT SYSTEM THAT HELPS HOLD THE OCEAN BOTTOM IN PLACE. SINCE SEAGRASS GROWS TALL, IT CAN ALSO LESSEN OCEAN CURRENTS THAT SWEEP ACROSS THE OCEAN BOTTOM.

Green sea turtles also help support healthy seagrass beds that provide nurseries for young sea creatures, or places where other sea creatures can find shelter and grow.

Seagrasses are known as the "lungs of the sea." They give off necessary oxygen for the ecosystem. Unfortunately, in the last few decades, there has been a noticeable loss of seagrass. Scientists think this may be because there are fewer sea turtles. Untrimmed seagrass becomes unhealthy. Overgrown seagrasses can't grow across the sea floor. Overgrown seagrass can also keep ocean currents from flowing correctly.

If green sea turtle populations continue to decline, it may lead to their ecological extinction. A species is considered ecologically extinct when it doesn't have enough individuals to properly perform its role in an ecosystem. Eventually, the whole ecosystem can collapse, or fail.

A 2020 report from the United Nations (UN) said that 7 percent of seagrass meadow **habitat** is being lost worldwide per year.

AT HOME IN THE SEAGRASS

SEAGRASS DOESN'T ONLY PROVIDE OXYGEN TO THE OCEAN ECOSYSTEM. IT PROVIDES HOMES, HIDING PLACES, AND BREEDING AREAS FOR MANY TYPES OF SEA CREATURES, INCLUDING CRUSTACEANS, SHELLFISH, AND DIFFERENT KINDS OF FISH. WITHOUT GREEN SEA TURTLES TO MAINTAIN THE SEAGRASS, MANY OCEAN SPECIES, OR KINDS OF ANIMALS, WILL SUFFER.

LIFE CYCLE OF A SEA TURTLE

In the wild, green sea turtles can live more than 80 years. Green sea turtles start their lives in eggs buried in nests on the shore. They make their way to the ocean as small babies called hatchlings. Male sea turtles stay in the water their whole lives and females usually return to land only to lay eggs.

Green sea turtles don't have offspring, or babies, until they're between 20 and 50 years old. A lot can happen to a turtle between the time it hatches and when it's old enough to have offspring of its own. In fact, scientists believe that only 1 in 1,000 green sea turtles will survive into adulthood.

IT ALL BEGINS WITH AN EGG

EVERY TWO TO THREE YEARS, A FEMALE SEA TURTLE CAN LAY ABOUT 110 EGGS PER NEST. SHE'LL LAY NEW BUNCHES OF EGGS IN NEW NESTS ABOUT EVERY TWO WEEKS FOR SEVERAL MONTHS. EGGS STAY WARM IN THE SAND, THEN BABY TURTLES HATCH. THEY MUST MAKE THEIR WAY TO THE WATER, WHICH IS A VERY DANGEROUS JOURNEY.

If you ever see turtle eggs on a beach, you must leave them alone. Harming a turtle nest can keep those eggs from hatching and the baby turtles from beginning their lives in the sea.

POLLUTION AND CLIMATE CHANGE

Pollution is when people put harmful things into the air, water, and land. Trash in the oceans and on beaches harms sea turtles. They can become tangled in fishing nets. Plastic straws and bags look like food to a green sea turtle.

Global warming—a rise in global temperatures—is caused by human activity, such as burning fuels including coal. Global warming is part of climate change, which is causing polar ice to melt and sea levels to rise. That means that there are fewer beach areas for greens to use as nesting sites. Warmer ocean waters may also confuse greens as they migrate. Climate change also causes worse natural **disasters**, such as hurricanes, which can damage turtle nesting places.

THE FUTURE IS FEMALE

THE TEMPERATURE OF THE SAND AROUND GREEN TURTLE EGGS DETERMINES IF BABY TURTLES, CALLED HATCHLINGS, WILL BE MALE OR FEMALE. HIGHER TEMPERATURES LEAD TO MORE FEMALES. WARMER SAND CAUSED BY GLOBAL WARMING CAUSES AN IMBALANCE THAT CAN AFFECT TURTLE POPULATIONS WHEN IT'S TIME FOR ADULTS TO BREED.

Plastic bags are particularly dangerous for young greens, which may confuse the bags for jellyfish.

HARMING NESTING SITES

Green sea turtles have many adaptations that help them survive in the water. Their strong flippers help them swim up to 22 miles (35.4 km) per hour. They can stay underwater for up to seven hours by slowing their heart rate to save oxygen.

Unfortunately, the features that make greens great swimmers cause them to move slowly on land, making them easier targets for predators and humans. As more beachfront properties are built, beaches become smaller and busier. People may hurt eggs or hatchlings by walking or driving over them. Green turtles may also avoid nesting on beaches where there's lots of noise and human activity.

BEACH TRASH TROUBLES

TRASH AND OTHER OBJECTS, SUCH AS CHAIRS, ON A BEACH MAY GET IN A FEMALE TURTLE'S WAY AS SHE COMES ON SHORE TO LAY HER EGGS. THIS MAY CAUSE HER TO TURN AROUND AND HEAD BACK INTO THE OCEAN. IF GREENS DO NEST ON A BUSY BEACH, IT'S IMPORTANT FOR PEOPLE TO LEAVE THEM ALONE AND PICK UP LITTER.

Beachfront development has reduced the number of peaceful nesting sites for greens. How can a turtle get to their nesting sites with so many chairs, umbrellas, and people in the way?

Unhatched turtle eggs add important **nutrients** to the sand, which helps plants grow on sand dunes. This creates more stable shorelines. These plants, as well as turtle eggs, also provide food for many species, or kinds of animals, that live on the beach. Even the smallest sea turtles can make a difference in their beach ecosystem.

After they hatch, it may take up to a week for baby greens to dig out of their nest. Hatchlings use moonlight to guide them to the ocean. Other sources of light, such as homes or hotels, near a nesting beach may confuse hatchlings. They may move inland, where they'll often die.

SWIM FRENZY

IF HATCHLINGS ARE LUCKY ENOUGH TO REACH THE OCEAN, THEY BEGIN WHAT IS KNOWN AS A "SWIM FRENZY." THEY SWIM AS FAST AS THEY CAN FOR 24 TO 48 HOURS UNTIL THEY REACH SAFER, DEEPER WATERS. UNFORTUNATELY, SHARKS AND BIRDS WILL GO AFTER HATCHLINGS IN THE OCEAN.

In some places in Central America and Asia, people dig up and eat green sea turtle eggs.

HELPING TURTLES RECOVER

Because of human actions and natural events, green sea turtles can become injured. Sometimes turtles are hit by a boat. Other turtles can become sick. Fibropapillomatosis (FP) is a disease that causes **tumors** to grow on the flippers, neck, and face of many kinds of sea turtles. Green sea turtles are most affected by this disease.

Many hurt or injured green sea turtles die, but some are taken to **rehabilitation** facilities. These exist at zoos, aquariums, and other organizations around the world. The goal of turtle rehabilitation is to make sick or injured sea turtles healthy enough to return to their home in the wild.

NO RETURN TO THE WILD

SOME SEA TURTLES DON'T HEAL WELL ENOUGH TO BE RELEASED BACK TO THE WILD. THESE TURTLES SOMETIMES REMAIN AT THE REHABILITATION FACILITY SO THEIR HEALTH CAN BE WATCHED AND THEIR SPECIES CAN BE STUDIED. THEY HELP SCIENTISTS LEARN MORE ABOUT HOW PEOPLE ARE HARMING WILDLIFE. THEY'RE SOMETIMES USED TO TEACH AND RAISE AWARENESS ABOUT THIS SPECIES.

Scientists aren't sure what causes fibropapillomatosis in sea turtles, but it occurs more in places with increased human activity.

CONSERVATION EFFORTS

Green sea turtle awareness has come a long way in the past century. Conservationist Archie Carr spent more than 50 years studying sea turtles, starting in the 1930s. He founded conservation groups and wrote many articles and books about green sea turtles.

Green sea turtles were listed under the Endangered Species Act (ESA) in 1978 as threatened or endangered, depending on their location. The ESA makes it illegal to buy, sell, or move sea turtles and turtle products. Conservation efforts include hatcheries where green sea turtle eggs are kept safe. The baby greens are released into the ocean once they've hatched.

PROTECTED...OR NOT?

GREEN SEA TURTLES ARE LISTED AS ENDANGERED OR THREATENED BASED ON POPULATIONS OR DIFFERENT LAWS. IN SOME PLACES, THEY STILL DON'T HAVE ANY LOCAL PROTECTION AT ALL. THE CONVENTION ON INTERNATIONAL TRADE IN ENDANGERED SPECIES (CITES) BEGAN TO PROTECT THEM IN 1975 INTERNATIONALLY AS THEY MIGRATE.

THREATS TO GREEN SEA TURTLES

- habitat loss
- global warming
- illegal trade and use
- accidental capture when fishing
- pollution

In the United States, the U.S. Fish and Wildlife Service protects green sea turtles on land, while the National Marine Fisheries Service protects them in the water.

GREEN SEA TURTLES TODAY

The U.S. government protects green sea turtles on its own land and in its own waters. But private organizations also do a lot of work to conserve this species. They educate the public, crack down on illegal activity, and keep nesting beaches clean and peaceful for greens. They also work with government agencies to set up protected lands.

To guess the number of greens in a population, scientists have counted the number of nesting females or groups of eggs on a beach. This can be inaccurate, though, so they're working on new methods of estimation. Scientists believe that populations in much of the Pacific grew or stayed the same between 2002 and 2015. Populations also seem to be steady or growing in the Atlantic coast areas of the United States.

The Archie Carr National Wildlife Refuge in Florida is one place where green sea turtles are protected.

THE SEA TURTLE CONSERVANCY

THE SEA TURTLE CONSERVANCY, FOUNDED IN 1959, WORKS TO SAVE SEA TURTLES FROM EXTINCTION. IT'S THE WORLD'S OLDEST SEA TURTLE RESEARCH AND CONSERVATION GROUP. THIS ORGANIZATION WORKS TO RESEARCH, EDUCATE, AND PROTECT SEA TURTLES AND THEIR HABITATS AROUND THE WORLD. IT HAS UNCOVERED MUCH OF WHAT WE KNOW ABOUT SEA TURTLES AND THEIR STRUGGLES.

YOU CAN SAVE SEA TURTLES

Conservation efforts have made a big difference in green sea turtle populations. Green sea turtles still need a lot of help to grow their numbers, though.

There are things you can do to help. If you live near a beach where sea turtles nest, you can turn off, block, or dim the lights around your home at night so nesting females and hatchlings don't get confused. If you visit a beach, keep an eye out for possible nests and hatchlings so you don't walk on them. You can also help to clean up beaches. Finally, educate others about green sea turtles and why they need our help.

REDUCE, REUSE, RECYCLE

WHAT IF YOU DON'T LIVE NEAR A BEACH? YOU CAN STILL HELP GREEN SEA TURTLES AND THEIR HABITATS. USE FEWER CHEMICALS IN THINGS YOU USE EVERY DAY, LIKE SHAMPOO AND LAUNDRY SOAP. REDUCE THE AMOUNT OF TRASH YOU PRODUCE. TRY NOT TO USE SINGLE-USE PLASTICS, SUCH AS BAGS AND STRAWS. IF YOU HAVE TO USE PLASTIC, RECYCLE IT RESPONSIBLY.

If you see a green sea turtle, it's important that you don't bother it. Respect its space. You might just save its life.

GLOSSARY

algae: Plantlike living things without roots or stems that live in water.

breed: To produce young.

conservation: Efforts to care for the natural world.

decline: To become less in amount.

disaster: Something that happens suddenly and causes much suffering and loss.

graze: To feed on plants or algae.

habitat: The natural place where an animal or plant lives.

nutrient: Something taken in by a plant or animal that helps it grow and stay healthy.

overexploit: To use a renewable resource to the point where it starts to run out.

rehabilitation: The process of making something healthy again.

subtropical: Describing places near tropical, or warm and wet, regions.

tragic: Describing something that is extremely unfortunate or upsetting.

tumor: A growth of cells in the body that isn't normal.

FOR MORE INFORMATION

Books

Johnson, Rebecca. *Grace the Green Sea Turtle*. New York, NY: Windmill Books, 2018.

Lawrence, Ellen. *A Sea Turtle's Life*. New York, NY: Bearport Publishing, 2017.

London, Martha. *Saving Green Sea Turtles*. Lake Elmo, MN: Focus Readers, 2021.

Websites

A Guide to Climate Change for Kids
climatekids.nasa.gov/kids-guide-to-climate-change/
Learn more about climate change with NASA's helpful guide.

DK Find Out! Sea Turtles
www.dkfindout.com/us/animals-and-nature/reptiles/sea-turtles/
Learn more about the different body parts of sea turtles that help them survive in their ocean habitats.

Green Sea Turtle Facts!
www.natgeokids.com/uk/discover/animals/sea-life/green-sea-turtle-facts/
Find more fun facts about green sea turtles with National Geographic Kids.

INDEX